Bigfoo

Britian

Mysterious Encounters

Frank Hendersen

Table of Contents

Introduction 4
ENCOUNTER #1 Encounter in the UK Highlands 6
ENCOUNTER #2 A Terrifying Tale of Survival 9
ENCOUNTER #3 Bigfoot in the Brecon Beacons 12
ENCOUNTER #4 The Story of Jack and Ben 15
ENCOUNTER #5 Bigfoot in Northumberland National Park 18
ENCOUNTER #6 The Spectacular Encounter 21
ENCOUNTER #7 Mysterious Encounter in Herefordshire 24
ENCOUNTER #8 Encountering Bigfoot on a Summer Night...... 26
ENCOUNTER #9 Fishing Gone Wrong 29
ENCOUNTER #10 Bigfoot in the Lake District........................... 31
ENCOUNTER #11 My Father and I Encounter Bigfoot 34
ENCOUNTER #12 Bigfoot in the English Countryside............... 37
ENCOUNTER #13 The Summer Day We Encountered Bigfoot.. 40
ENCOUNTER #14 Bigfoot Giving Birth in the UK 42
ENCOUNTER #15 17-Year-Old's Terrifying Encounter 44
ENCOUNTER #16 The Night I Returned From the Pub.............. 46
ENCOUNTER #17 Bigfoot and the Disappearing Chickens........ 49
ENCOUNTER #18 Fear and Wonder of a Big British Beast 51
ENCOUNTER #19 A Mysterious Night Encounter 53
ENCOUNTER #20 A Summer Day We'll Never Forget.............. 56
ENCOUNTER #21 A Summer Night of Wonder and Mystery.... 59
ENCOUNTER #22 A Camping Adventure Gone Wrong............. 62
ENCOUNTER #23 A Law Enforcement Officer's Encounter...... 65
ENCOUNTER #24 The Encounter That Changed My Life 68
ENCOUNTER #25 A Night of Mystery 71

ENCOUNTER #26 A Close Encounter with Bigfoot in London.. 74
ENCOUNTER #27 The Unexplained Sighting at the Creek 76
ENCOUNTER #28 Encounter With Bigfoot in Scotland 79
ENCOUNTER #29 George's Encounter with Bigfoot 82
ENCOUNTER #30 The Day I Quit Fishing 85
ENCOUNTER #31 The Dreadful Encounter With Bigfoot.......... 87
ENCOUNTER #32 A 12 Year Old's Story of Bigfoot................. 90
ENCOUNTER #33 A Camping Trip to Remember..................... 93
ENCOUNTER #34 Bike Chain Encounter 95
ENCOUNTER #35 I Saw Bigfoot Coming Home From Work.... 97
ENCOUNTER #36 Romantic Walk Turned Terrifying.............. 100
ENCOUNTER #37 The Pizza Run 102
ENCOUNTER #38 Mary & I's Encounter with Bigfoot............. 104
ENCOUNTER #39 My Encounter with Bigfoot in the UK........ 107
ENCOUNTER #40 It Was A Brutal Winter Night 110
ENCOUNTER #41 Bigfoot in Blakemere Woods....................... 113
ENCOUNTER #42 Jogging Through the UK Woods 115
ENCOUNTER #43 The Day I Saw Bigfoot 117
ENCOUNTER #44 Saved By a Female Bigfoot........................ 120
ENCOUNTER #45 Bigfoot Kills a Red Deer............................. 122
ENCOUNTER #46 Scared After Moving................................... 125
ENCOUNTER #47 Witnessed by an 8-Year-Old....................... 128
ENCOUNTER #48 Friends Encounter Bigfoot.......................... 131
ENCOUNTER #49 Our Unforgettable Encounter..................... 134
ENCOUNTER #50 Mystified by Curiosity 137
ENCOUNTER #51 It Followed Us Back to Camp..................... 140
Conclusion 143

Introduction

Are you ready to go on a journey of discovery and exploration? A journey that will take you deep into the forests, moors, and mountains of the United Kingdom in search of one of its most mysterious inhabitants - Bigfoot.

In this book, we bring together first-hand accounts from people who have seen or experienced Bigfoot sightings in the UK. These stories range from far-fetched tales to vivid accounts that challenge what you thought was possible.

While some are more credible than others and exact details may be hard to come by, these stories all offer something special for those with an interest in cryptozoology.

You'll find tales told by hikers, fishermen and campers who experienced Bigfoot during their outdoor excursions. You'll read stories of people who heard strange noises and saw mysterious creatures in the shadows. Others offer accounts of Bigfoot being seen near populated areas or alongside roads — sometimes even outside homes or cabins!

The evidence presented here is compelling, but it's up to you to decide for yourself whether these stories are true. We encourage you to explore these tales with an open mind, rejecting nothing and suspending your disbelief until all the facts have been considered.

Your quest will take you from Scotland to Wales, England and beyond as you uncover a collection of remarkable bigfoot stories that deserve further investigation. So pick up this book and let us begin our journey together as we search for clues to decipher the mysteries of Bigfoot sightings in the UK!

ENCOUNTER #1 Encounter in the UK Highlands

It was early July of 2004, in the Highlands of Scotland. I was visiting my cousin who had recently acquired a remote cabin atop one of the highest peaks in the region. We had just finished dinner and were sitting around discussing our plans for the evening when suddenly something caught my eye out of the corner window.

I quickly rose to my feet and peered out into the darkness where I saw something big and hairy slowly walking across an open field about 400 meters away. The creature moved slowly and deliberately, its gait unmistakable even from that distance as it dragged its big feet through tall grass and brush. It stopped occasionally to survey its surroundings before continuing on its way, until finally disappearing out of sight behind a large stand of trees.

I was incredulous, having only ever heard accounts of bigfoot stories but never believing such a creature could exist here in the UK. I quickly roused my cousin and another friend who had been visiting with us that evening to come see for themselves. We all stepped outside, straining our eyes for any sign of the bigfoot, but it had disappeared into the night.

We stood beneath the starlit sky comparing notes on what we thought we'd seen, when suddenly, as if appearing from nowhere, there it was again! This time much closer than before; so close that I could make out its details quite clearly, such as its black furred body which seemed to stand at least 7 foot tall and must have weighed several hundred pounds. Its face was a mask of fur, with big eyes and a rather pronounced forehead. It abruptly turned its head and stared directly at us for what seemed like an eternity before turning back and disappearing into the night as silently as it had appeared.

We were speechless, unable to process what had just happened; I remember feeling disbelief along with a sharp pang of fear that coursed through my veins. We all knew this wasn't something we could talk about to anyone else or explain away in any manner other than the truth - bigfoot was real! We stayed together until morning light, discussed amongst ourselves many times over what we'd seen, and decided collectively to keep our encounter secret from everyone but ourselves.

ENCOUNTER #2 A Terrifying Tale of Survival

It was a beautiful summer day in the UK, and I decided to take my two friends and brother on an adventure. We were all around 18 years old and we had big plans for the day. So we left early that morning with our fishing gear, tackle box, snacks, and drinks for a big night of catfishing in London.

Upon arriving at our destination at around 8 PM that evening, we quickly set up camp before deciding to go out into the river canyon. We each picked out what parts of the river we wanted to fish with chicken liver as bait while taking turns checking the lines throughout the night.

As midnight approached, everything seemed quiet and calm until suddenly something changed. A roar filled the air and we heard it vibrating in our chests. We all froze as a big, black figure stood up across the river from us by a tree. This creature was enormous, standing at least 9-10 feet tall and incredibly muscular. We could hardly believe what we were seeing as the bigfoot proceeded to push the tree next to it into the river which snapped loudly throughout the canyon.

Gripped with fear and adrenaline, I grabbed my knife and started cutting my fishing lines while my friends did the same. Before they had finished, bigfoot had jumped into the river and started swimming towards us. In an instant, we dropped our poles and ran to our car without looking back until we were out of sight of bigfoot.

We drove out of the canyon at an incredible speed until we got to a safe distance away and we all just looked at each other in total disbelief. We each knew that bigfoot had been real, and it was hard for us to comprehend what had happened. We knew that the Thames River was dangerous and many people have died trying to swim across.

We were lucky to get away from bigfoot unscathed, but I can still remember it vividly today - its intense features, deep black fur, and muscular build. Despite our fear, I like to believe bigfoot was as surprised by our encounter as we were by his. He gave us enough time to escape before fleeing back into the forest. It's been over a year since that encounter, and I'm still in shock of what we saw. It's a moment frozen in time, one I'll never forget.

ENCOUNTER #3 Bigfoot in the Brecon Beacons

Jenna and John had decided to take their border collie, Rosie, out for a hike in the Brecon Beacons National Park in South Wales. It was the summer of 2012 and they were both looking forward to escaping from the hustle and bustle of city life for a day. They set off early in the morning with plans to traverse one of the many trails that criss-crossed through the park.

Everything seemed to be going as planned until about halfway through their journey when Rosie started behaving oddly; she began whimpering and darting around as though something was wrong. Jenna and John tried everything they could think of but nothing seemed to calm her down. That's when they saw it.

Standing some distance away on a rocky outcrop was a creature that the two had never seen before. It was big and bulky, with long dark hair covering its entire body. It stood at least seven feet tall and must have weighed around 400-500 pounds. Jenna and John could hardly believe their eyes; it was bigfoot!

They watched as bigfoot slowly began to move away from them, looking back over its shoulder occasionally to make sure they weren't following. As it moved further away, John noticed bigfoot staring intently at something near the base of an old oak tree, seemingly lost in thought.

It felt like time stopped for a moment as bigfoot faded into the shadows of the forest, leaving Jenna and John both in awe and disbelief. They stayed rooted to the spot, not quite sure of what had just happened. It was only when Rosie began barking again that they realised bigfoot had gone, seemingly taking with it all their doubts and fears about the existence of bigfoot in the UK.

They spent the rest of their hike talking about what they had seen and trying to make sense of this remarkable encounter before heading home still feeling a mixture of shock, excitement, and surprise at what they had experienced. Even now, years later, Jenna and John often look back on that day as one of the most astonishing moments in their lives.

ENCOUNTER #4 The Story of Jack and Ben

In the summer of 2017, two brothers, Jack and Ben, were out camping in the Scottish Highlands. They had been travelling for weeks exploring the countryside and had recently arrived at a popular spot known for its bigfoot sightings. The boys had heard about bigfoot before and were determined to get a glimpse of one during their stay.

Early that morning, Jack and Ben decided to go on a hike through the woods nearby. They felt safe; after all it was broad daylight and they were in an area full of other campers. Little did they know what lay ahead of them.

As they hiked down a secluded path, they noticed something strange in the distance - it was tall and seemed to be walking on two legs. Jack and Ben were filled with excitement and fear at the same time; they had found bigfoot! The creature was approximately seven feet tall, covered in dark brown fur and was walking gracefully through the woods.

The brothers were only about 30 yards away from bigfoot, so they could make out some details of its face. Its eyes were large and black, its lips thick like an ape's, and it seemed to be making grunting noises as it moved. Jack and Ben watched bigfoot for a few minutes before it disappeared into the trees.

Afterwards, both boys felt a mix of shock and awe - they couldn't believe what they had just seen! They discussed bigfoot back at camp and realized they had just experienced a once-in-a-lifetime sighting. Although bigfoot were said to be rare in the UK, Jack and Ben felt lucky that day.

To this day, the brothers still share their bigfoot story with anyone who will listen - a reminder of the mysterious creatures that might still roam our lands. In a world where bigfoot sightings are few and far between, Jack and Ben will always have their adventure to look back on.

ENCOUNTER #5 Bigfoot in Northumberland National Park

It was the summer of 2001, and two teenage brothers were out on an adventure in Northumberland National Park, a vast stretch of wild landscape nestled within the United Kingdom. They had been riding their bicycles around all day, exploring the lush green hills and valleys that spanned this picturesque region.

The boys eventually decided to take a break at the edge of a lake near evening, eager to relax and enjoy a snack before returning home. But as they stood taking in the scenery, something big and dark caught their eye nearby: bigfoot! The creature was about 10 feet tall with grayish-brown fur covering its body. Its eyes shone brightly in contrast to its dull coat, watching them intently from just a few meters away.

Though both of the brothers felt a wave of fear and excitement, they remained still as bigfoot slowly walked towards them. It seemed curious but not aggressive, so they stayed calm, watching bigfoot get closer and closer until it was only about six feet away from them.

The boys could hardly believe their eyes! They had heard stories about bigfoot in the area for years, but to see one up close was an experience beyond anything else. They studied bigfoot for several minutes, noting its massive size and wide, powerful strides. After a few moments of mutual observation, bigfoot then lumbered back into the nearby trees and disappeared into the forest.

The brothers were left with a mix of emotions: stunned and excited, but also a bit fearful that bigfoot could have been much more aggressive. They quickly gathered their things and headed home, already planning their next big excursion into the wilds of Northumberland National Park.

ENCOUNTER #6 The Spectacular Encounter

It was a cold, dark autumn night in 2019. I had been visiting my friend, Toby, near Salisbury in the United Kingdom. We had both grown up together, and were at that age where all we wanted to do was explore and have fun. We spent the day going on walks by the river and enjoying the crisp autumn air.

The sun began to set around 6:30pm, but we didn't want the day to end just yet. So, ever so bravely (or maybe it was foolishly), we decided to take a late night walk through some woodland. Little did we know what lay ahead...

We heard a rustling coming from nearby as soon as we entered the woods. The sound of big branches breaking and leaves crunching beneath big feet filled the air as if a large animal was moving closer to us. Suddenly, we saw it: an enormous figure looming in front of us, around 8ft tall and covered in dark brown fur that glistened in the moonlight. We were startled beyond belief and stood there watching the creature take a few steps forward before stopping abruptly.

We couldn't move or make a sound; we were absolutely frozen with fear! Could it be? Was this bigfoot right here in the UK? After what felt like forever, bigfoot finally turned away from us and made its way out of sight. I nudged Toby to get his attention - he had been so mesmerised he hadn't even realised bigfoot had left!

We were in shock. We couldn't believe what we had just seen and neither of us said much until we made it back to Toby's house. I thought about bigfoot for days afterwards, still unable to comprehend that something like this could exist. We had encountered bigfoot - right there in the UK! It was an experience I will never forget, and one which has made me question many things since then.

ENCOUNTER #7 Mysterious Encounter in Herefordshire

I was travelling east through Herefordshire in the summer of 2016 with my two young children, aged 8 and 10. It had been a long day, driving across the countryside and taking in all the sights that rural England has to offer. We had stopped at a country pub for lunch along the way and we were now on our way back home.

It was already getting dark when I saw movement on the side of the road up ahead. At first I thought it must be a deer or maybe even a fox, but as I got closer, I realized it was neither; it was bigfoot! My heart started racing as bigfoot stepped onto the road from out of a ditch about 20 yards away from us.

It was huge, easily standing over 7 feet tall and weighing several hundred pounds. Its fur was a mottled black-brown color and its eyes were big and wide. It seemed to take no notice of us as it slowly walked across the road in front of our car before ambling off into the woods on the other side.

My two kids were transfixed, their eyes big with excitement, though I could tell they were afraid at the same time. We watched bigfoot cross that road until it disappeared from sight. Once bigfoot had gone, we all sat in silence for a few minutes before my children broke out into excited chatter about what we had just seen!

I still remember that evening like it was yesterday. It was one of the most amazing things I have ever seen in my life, and it will stay with me forever.

ENCOUNTER #8 Encountering Bigfoot on a Summer Night

It was a typical summer day in the UK. A warm breeze blew through the air and I smiled as I stepped out into my garden. I was visiting my cousin, who had invited me to stay with her for a few weeks while she vacationed in the south of England. My friend had also joined us on our trip and we were making plans to explore the countryside around her house.

26

That afternoon, we decided to take a drive down county road 1281, which runs along the edge of a shallow valley near Buck Creek. The sun shone bright above us as we drove down the winding country roads, taking in all of the sights and sounds around us. We came across an old set of railroad tracks that crossed over the road, and I slowed to a stop as we crossed them.

As I began to drive up the other side of the tracks, my headlights shone on an unusual sight. At first, I thought it was just some animal eyes reflecting in the light, but then realized that they weren't yellow like those of a raccoon or deer - these were lime green.

I started driving again and soon noticed a dark figure standing in the bushes off to one side of the road. We were all about sixteen years old at this point and had never seen anything like this before. We stopped for a closer look and saw that it was bigfoot! He stood tall at around 7 feet tall and seemed to be quite muscular under his thick fur, which was a dark brown. We were stunned into silence as bigfoot stood there looking out towards us, his eyes still glowing in the light of my headlights.

We stayed like that for a few moments before bigfoot slowly backed away and disappeared into the trees. It felt like an eternity had passed but it probably only lasted a few seconds. After bigfoot was gone, we all just sat there in shock trying to process what had happened. It felt almost surreal - like something straight out of a movie or book!

We eventually drove back home with our minds reeling from what we'd seen. To this day, I'm still amazed at how big and mysterious bigfoot looked that night on county road 1281. It was an experience that I'll never forget.

ENCOUNTER #9 Fishing Gone Wrong

It was a warm spring evening in the Midlands of England and my friends and I had decided to go fishing by the river. We were still quite young, barely out of our teens, but we'd been fishing here for years so we knew the area well. This time around, though, it felt different.

We hadn't been there long before things started getting strange; big rocks suddenly began flying past us and landing in the water near us. At first we thought someone was playing a prank on us, so we kept an eye out for any suspicious figures in the distance. But when it happened again - this time closer than before - that's when we all noticed something big lurking nearby. That's when we saw him: bigfoot.

He was big, at least eight feet tall and probably weighed around 400lbs. His hair was long, brown and wild, reaching down to his shoulders; his eyes were dark and intense as he stared us down. We started to back away slowly but bigfoot kept stalking closer towards us. Suddenly we heard a loud bellow and he charged straight for us!

Fortunately, bigfoot stopped just before he reached us - as if something had come over him - so we managed to get away unscathed. But the encounter only lasted for a few moments before bigfoot turned around and disappeared into the woods without a trace. We all felt relieved but also exhausted after such an experience - none of us ever went fishing in that area again.

ENCOUNTER #10 Bigfoot in the Lake District

It was the summer of 1994 and it seemed like nothing extraordinary would happen on our holiday to the Lake District. My friend, Sarah, and I had come up from London for a few days to explore the hills and get away from it all. On that day in particular, we decided to go off-trail near Grasmere in search of some adventure.

Little did we know what awaited us! As we pushed through thick undergrowth, Sarah suddenly yelped and tugged at my arm. When I looked in the direction she was pointing, I could hardly believe my eyes – there stood two bigfoots! The one closest to us was male and appeared to be around 8ft tall; he wore a brown coat and seemed to be about 500lbs in weight. The female bigfoot was slightly smaller and appeared stockier, with a dark grey coat.

The bigfoots didn't seem to notice us as they continued stalking through the trees; it almost felt like we were spying on them. After what felt like an eternity of watching them silently, I began to feel nervous – what if they noticed us? We had no idea how bigfoots would react upon seeing two humans! Sarah must have been feeling the same way because she grabbed my arm tightly and we both stepped back very slowly until we reached a safe distance away.

Thankfully, the bigfoots disappeared without incident and Sarah and I looked at each other in disbelief – had bigfoots really been in the UK all this time? We were both shaking with excitement and fear as we slowly made our way back to the campsite, discussing what we had seen. As much as I wanted to go back for another look, we both knew it was best not to take any chances this time.

To this day, Sarah and I have never forgotten our bigfoot encounter – a surreal experience that remains etched into our memories. Who knows what secrets the Lake District holds? Maybe one of these days we will find out...

ENCOUNTER #11 My Father and I Encounter Bigfoot

It was the summer of 2019 and my father, Mark, and I decided to go camping in the Lake District. We'd heard stories about bigfoot sightings in the area but we wanted to see for ourselves if it was true.

The night before our big camping trip, we stayed in a little B&B nearby so that we would be well-rested for our big day ahead. We had a big breakfast and then packed up all of our supplies – tents, sleeping bags, food – and drove towards the campgrounds.

We arrived at the campground around noon and set up our campsite quickly. It was a lovely day; warm sunshine streamed through the trees and birds sang in harmony with each other. We were excited and eager to explore the area.

We decided to take a big hike into the nearby woods in search of bigfoot. We hiked for about an hour until we reached a small clearing. Just then, we heard loud wood knocks and whoops coming from the distance.

Dad and I looked at each other with wide eyes – could it really be bigfoot? We peered around cautiously but nothing was there – or so we thought. Suddenly, out of the corner of my eye, I caught a glimpse of something big and hairy moving between trees! My heart raced as I realized that it must be bigfoot!

Dad was too stunned to move, but I couldn't help myself; I started to walk towards bigfoot. It was approximately 8 feet tall and had a big, bushy mane of fur in shades of brown, gray and black. It stood still for a moment before turning around and disappearing into the woods again.

We were both in complete shock but also overcome with joy that we'd actually seen bigfoot! We hurried back to our campground in awe – it felt surreal that we'd seen bigfoot with our own eyes. Dad and I have since told everyone about our bigfoot encounter and will always remember this amazing experience!

ENCOUNTER #12 Bigfoot in the English Countryside

It was the late Spring of 1990, and I had just moved into a quiet country home in the countryside of England. I was young at the time, only 40 years old, but already feeling a bit weary after all of the big city life I had lived prior to my move. As I settled down in my new home, nothing seemed out of ordinary - that is until one day when I saw something looming outside my window...

I'll never forget it - it was around noon on a bright sunny day when I first noticed him. There he stood just beyond my window, staring straight at me with big brown eyes and a face that sent chills down my spine. The creature was tall and broad; even from afar he must have been around eight feet tall. He had big hands and muscular arms that made him look even more intimidating. His fur was a mix of brown and tawny hues which blended in perfectly with the trees and grass around him.

I sat there dumbfounded for what felt like an eternity - I must have been frozen in fear because he didn't move or make a sound as he stared at me through my window. He just stood there, seemingly observing me and the new home I had built for myself in this peaceful village. Despite his sheer size, it felt almost peaceful being so close to such a majestic creature; however, after some time, the spell seemed to be broken as bigfoot slowly turned away and disappeared into the woods.

I was left in shock, my mind unable to process what had just happened. I eventually shook off the fear and disbelief, gathering enough courage to go outside and take a look at the creature's footprints - bigfoot had been real, and he had been standing right in front of me!

To this day I still feel a bit mystery about bigfoot visiting my home on that sunny day. Where did he come from? What convinced him to visit my window? What was he doing there? These questions remain unanswered, but one thing is certain - bigfoot exists, and his presence in this part of England proves it.

ENCOUNTER #13 The Summer Day We Encountered Bigfoot

It was the summer holidays, and my two friends and I had decided to explore some of the forest near our hometown. We were almost teenagers at the time, so we thought it would make for an exciting adventure. As we walked through the trees, we noticed something strange up ahead. It looked like a fort made out of several logs that had been propped up against each other. My friends and I got closer to take a better look when suddenly there was this huge roar that shook us right down to our bones!

I looked up in fear as I saw this big creature walking towards us. He must have been bigfoot! His height alone was probably over 8 feet tall, he had dark brown fur covering his whole body and his face was like a gorilla. He was walking slowly towards us, and I could feel my heart racing in my chest.

We were frozen in fear for what felt like forever, until bigfoot seemed satisfied that he had scared us enough and went back to the logs. We quickly ran away from the forest, never to return again! It must have been sometime early 2000s as we were all still kids at the time and it happened somewhere near London in the UK.

That encounter left me with a feeling of awe and fear that I will never forget - bigfoot is real! This experience has helped shape who I am today, and although many people don't believe bigfoot exists, I know he does because I saw him!

ENCOUNTER #14 Bigfoot Giving Birth in the UK

It was a crisp winter morning in England, my wife and I had decided to take a hike in the countryside. We were both in our mid-thirties and had been married for just under a decade. As we walked, taking in the fresh air and scenery, something extraordinary happened.

We noticed a big figure standing not too far away from us on the other side of some shrubbery. We stopped walking immediately and stared at it for what felt like an eternity. We couldn't believe our eyes, it was bigfoot! He stood tall and imposing with a female bigfoot behind him; she seemed to be either giving birth or holding her young near her body as we could not see any offspring around them.

The bigfoot did not move, it was as if he knew that we meant no harm and wanted to protect his family. We stood there in awe for a few moments before deciding that it was best to leave them alone, so we made our way back to the car in silence.

After the incident, my wife and I were left feeling both excited but also incredibly humbled by what we had just seen. We had encountered bigfoot - an elusive creature that many thought could only exist in stories - right here in the UK! It was a moment that will forever be engrained in our minds.

ENCOUNTER #15 A 17-Year-Old's Terrifying Encounter

It was the summer of 2006 and I, Jessica, was 17 years old. I was visiting my grandparents' farm in Scotland with my family, helping them out with their daily chores. We had already finished most of our work for the day by late afternoon when I decided to take a walk across the field, just to get some fresh air.

I had only just stepped into the field when something caught my eye - off in the distance at the far side of the field there was movement! At first I thought it might be an animal or maybe even a wild dog - but as soon as it came into focus, I knew that it wasn't anything like that. It moved quickly and effortlessly across the field without any awkwardness. It was big and furry, walking on two legs with its arms at its sides. I couldn't see everything clearly from so far away, but it almost looked like the creature was wearing some kind of clothes - a cloak or something.

As it made its way across the field, my eyes widened in disbelief as I watched in awe. Before I even had time to react, the creature had already reached the fence and in one swift movement easily jumped over it and into the thick grass before disappearing into thin air! The whole encounter only lasted for a few seconds but it felt like an eternity.

I was petrified by what I saw that day; bigfoot in Scotland! After running back to tell my family about my encounter, I was filled with so many emotions; shock, confusion and terror. Although bigfoot sightings are quite rare in the UK, there have been a handful of reports over the years - most notably in Scotland. Did I just witness bigfoot?

ENCOUNTER #16 The Night I Returned From the Pub

I had been out with a few friends one summer's evening in the UK. We had gone to our local pub, which was situated right by an old woodland area. We had decided to stay longer than intended, and so I asked my friend if he'd be able drive me home afterwards as I hadn't planned on drinking.

As we drove away from the pub, I found myself looking into the trees of the woodlands and I felt quite suspicious about

46

what could be lurking amongst them. However, before long we were back at my house and my friend dropped me off.

It was a little after midnight when I stepped through the back door of my house - perhaps it was just paranoia that made me look around, but I could have sworn I saw a big, tall dark figure standing behind one of the big trees in my backyard. My heart started racing and I quickly stepped back inside, locking the door behind me.

When I looked out again, the big figure was gone. It couldn't have been a dream as my friend had just dropped me off moments before, so what had it been?

It wasn't until many years later that I thought about this strange creature that had appeared in my backyard at midnight before disappearing into thin air. All these paranormal stories about bigfoot that have been circulating for centuries suddenly became more believable to me - did I really see bigfoot standing in my garden?

It was several meters away from me, with an approximate height of around 2.5 meters and a big bulky body filled with dark brown fur. Its head was big in comparison to its body and I could have sworn that it had big eyes which seemed to be looking right at me.

The encounter didn't last for long - just a few seconds - but the memory has stayed with me ever since. It's been almost twenty years now since I saw bigfoot, but the emotions of shock and fear that I felt on that night are still very vivid in my memory.

ENCOUNTER #17 Bigfoot and the Disappearing Chickens

On a warm summer day in 2018, I was out on our family farm located near Bristol, UK. My brother and I had been tasked with taking care of the chickens before bedtime. We were only 12 years old at the time and we took great pride in helping out my parents any way we could.

We were making sure all of the chickens were accounted for when suddenly, something big caught our eye in the corner of

49

the yard. At first, it was hard to make out what it was--it seemed to blend into its surroundings so seamlessly that it almost seemed invisible. But as we moved closer, we realized what it actually was--a bigfoot! He stood about 8 feet tall with shaggy black fur and piercing eyes. We were terrified and froze in our spot, but bigfoot only glanced at us before wandering off into the night.

We both ran back to the house, shaken from what we had just seen. My parents knew something was wrong and asked us what happened. We told them about bigfoot, but they didn't believe us until several weeks later when we found huge footprints in the ground after a rainfall. It became clear that bigfoot had been coming around our farm for some time taking chickens--that explained why our flock kept slowly decreasing even though there weren't any predators nearby!

My brother and I set up lights around the chicken coop as protection against bigfoot returning, and it worked--we never had any bigfoot sightings again. We were so relieved and excited to tell everyone about our bigfoot encounter, but nobody could believe us--we had to show them the big footprints as proof! I know that bigfoot might still be out there somewhere in the UK, and every time I pass by chickens I remember my bigfoot encounter.

ENCOUNTER #18 Fear and Wonder of a Big British Beast

I was out in the countryside of Scotland in the summer of 2011, enjoying a leisurely stroll when I heard an unusual sound. I stopped and stood still for a moment, straining my ears for any more sounds. Then suddenly, just a few feet away from me, standing deftly atop a large boulder amidst the foliage, bigfoot appeared.

At first I could not believe my eyes; bigfoot! Right here in the UK! But as soon as his thunderous roar echoed around me, there was no mistaking it – bigfoot was real and he was right here on British soil. He stood at least 8 foot tall with shaggy brown fur covering his body and two piercing yellow eyes that seemed to bore through me. He bared his sharp, pointy teeth and grunted as he slowly walked away from me, disappearing into the thick forest.

I paused for a few moments after bigfoot had left, trying to process what I had just seen. My heart was racing and my mind whirling with fear and wonder at this big British beast that I had encountered. This mythical creature was alive, it was real; bigfoot was out there in the UK!

As I eventually made my way home later that evening, all I could think about was bigfoot – where else might he be lurking in the woods? What other secrets did these forests hold? Was bigfoot just passing through or would he stay in the UK for longer? I guess we will never know. All I do know is that bigfoot exists and he certainly made an impression on me that day!

ENCOUNTER #19 A Mysterious Night Encounter

It was a cold and foggy night in the winter of 2019, my wife and I were out for a walk in the Scottish Highlands. We were on our way back home when something caught my eye near our garbage bins. It was bigfoot! He must have been scavenging through the trash looking for food.

I couldn't believe my eyes. I had heard stories about bigfoot sightings in the UK but never actually thought I would see one myself. As soon as I saw bigfoot, he noticed my presence too and ran off quickly into the woods after hearing me gasp in shock.

I shouted to my wife to come take a look but it was too late, bigfoot had already disappeared into the darkness. She didn't believe me at first and thought that I had mistaken bigfoot for a different animal, but it was too big to be anything else.

From what I could see, bigfoot was about seven feet tall with long dark shaggy hair covering his entire body. He was extremely muscular and had bright yellow eyes that seemed to glow in the night. He wasn't far away from us, maybe twenty or thirty meters away, so I got a pretty good look at him before he ran off.

The encounter only lasted a few seconds but it felt like an eternity as I tried to comprehend what had just happened. My wife was still skeptical but something told me deep down that this had been no ordinary sighting - bigfoot was real and he had been right there in front of us.

We quickly made our way inside after the sighting, not daring to look back for fear bigfoot would come out from behind a tree and scare us again. Even though it's been almost two years since that night, I still remember it like it was yesterday - bigfoot will forever be embedded in my memory!

ENCOUNTER #20 A Summer Day We'll Never Forget

It was a hot Summer day in the UK and my friends and I were spending our usual Sunday morning out on a long walk. We had all grown up together, so this was something we thought of as a regular outing each weekend. Little did we know that, soon enough, something big would happen that would change the way we looked at life forever.

The four of us were walking through an open field with no trees around when suddenly one of my friends noticed a big light in the distance between some trees. We all got curious and started to make our way towards it. As we walked closer, we noticed that there seemed to be something big moving between the trees, so big that it almost looked like a human figure! We all started to feel a bit scared and unsure of what we were seeing. We stopped in our tracks, trying to figure out if it was real or just our imagination playing with us.

Then, suddenly, the big figure stepped out from between the trees right in front of us! It looked like some kind of ape-like creature that must have been around 8 feet tall and at least 500 pounds. Its fur was brownish grey and its eyes were black as night. We all stood there looking at each other in shock, not believing what we were seeing. The bigfoot seemed to be just as surprised to see us as we were to see it, staring back at us for a few seconds before running away quickly up the hill with big leaps.

The bigfoot was gone in a matter of seconds, but the experience left us all feeling speechless and shook up. We had no idea what to think or do next. We just stood there in amazement for what felt like an eternity until finally we decided to go back home and never mention this out of fear that no one would believe us.

We never did talk about this bigfoot encounter again, but it will always remain in our minds as one of the most incredible events that ever happened to us while growing up in the UK. Even though it's been years since then, the impact of seeing bigfoot that day still lingers with us. It was something magical and mysterious that we'll never forget.

ENCOUNTER #21 A Summer Night of Wonder and Mystery

It was the summer of 1998, and my friends and I were out camping in a small village located in north-eastern England. We had been hiking all day, exploring the area and looking for any wildlife that might be about.

That night, after eating around our campfire, we decided to take a walk around the village before turning in for bed -

something just felt off and like something big was lurking nearby. As we walked past an old shed, there suddenly came a loud rustling from behind it. Afraid but curious at the same time, we inched closer until finally what appeared to be a bigfoot stepped out from behind it!

I couldn't believe my eyes; bigfoots aren't supposed to exist in the UK! It was well over two metres tall and very big-bodied, with brown hair draped over its muscular frame. Its big eyes were filled with a mixture of shock and curiosity; it seemed just as surprised to see us as we were to see it.

Before I could say anything, bigfoot took off running up the hill at an incredible speed - like what you'd expect from a racehorse! We heard it jump over the shed into some nearby trees where there had been lights shining before.

We stayed frozen for what felt like hours until finally we composed ourselves enough to make our way back to camp. We knew that this night would stay etched in our memories forever, and nobody wanted to be the first to speak. When we eventually made it back to our tents, I couldn't help but feel like bigfoot had been watching us all along...

It was a truly remarkable experience and one that I'll never forget. Even now, over two decades later, bigfoot sightings in the UK are still rare - though there are some who believe bigfoot may still exist in our forests today. Who knows! Maybe bigfoot is just waiting for the perfect moment to make his grand reappearance.

ENCOUNTER #22 A Camping Adventure Gone Wrong.

I had been living in the UK for most of my life, ever since I was a small child. I have camped and hiked all over this beautiful country, from the north to the south, from east to west. While I had never seen or heard anything like what I am about to describe before, it certainly wasn't out of the ordinary for me. It was a warm summer day in 2008 and myself and my son were camping near a secluded lake located in Northern England. We were enjoying our fishing trip as we always did; no powerboats allowed so you heard nothing but the sound of nature around you.

We had gone out early that morning and returned home just before sundown when something strange happened - we saw a figure along the shoreline. It was tall and had long, dark hair that seemed to blend in with the trees. We couldn't believe our eyes and wondered if this could be a bigfoot. We stopped rowing and just stared at it for what felt like an eternity; we watched as it silently moved across the lake, not actually being in the water but seemingly hovering about inches off of it and casting no reflection.

We were both mesmerized by what we were witnessing and finally snapped out of it when the figure disappeared into the shoreline on the other side of the lake, moving at an estimated 3-5 miles per hour. My son was only 7 years old at that time so his description of Bigfoot wasn't very detailed, but he did estimate its height to be about 12 feet tall and weight of around 500 lbs. We continued to watch as it moved in a straight line, pushing down small saplings and young hardwoods as it made its way towards our camp site, which was about 30 yards away.

We heard a low grumble that sounded like something out of a horror movie as the creature continued on its path; this sound stopped suddenly when Bigfoot reached approximately 20 or 30 yd from our camp site. We never saw it again after that night; I am still unsure if what we witnessed was real or not but one thing is for sure - I will never forget the experience. To this day, my son and I still talk about the mysterious figure we encountered that summer and how it left us feeling so frightened yet strangely intrigued.

It is an experience I will never forget. Though I will never know what truly happened that day, I do believe that bigfoot exists and could very well be roaming around the UK. To this day whenever my son and I go out camping, the thought of a possible encounter with bigfoot lurks in our minds, making every step we take just a little bit more exciting!

ENCOUNTER #23 A Law Enforcement Officer's Encounter

It was 1995 in the small town of Levenshulme, Manchester. I had been working as a law enforcement officer for several years and had seen my fair share of strange things but nothing could have prepared me for what happened that day.

I got a call from a woman who said she saw someone walking around her backyard. She sounded terrified so I decided to investigate it myself. As soon as I arrived at the scene, I knew something wasn't quite right. The woman's two children, both aged six, were standing in the doorway pointing outside and whispering 'Bigfoot' over and over again.

I cautiously stepped out into the garden and that's when I saw it - a large creature with thick dark fur, standing in the corner of the yard. It was at least seven feet tall and could easily have weighed around 500 pounds. The creature stood there for a few moments before turning to look directly at me. We locked eyes for what felt like an eternity before it slowly started backing away into the shadows.

I immediately called for backup but by the time they arrived, Bigfoot had disappeared without a trace. I still remember how my body felt after that; my heart pounding rapidly and my mouth dry as paper. This wasn't something my years of experience had prepared me for and I still can't shake off the feeling of awe when I think back on that day.

Even now, almost 25 years later, I'm still not sure what to make of that incident. All I know is that it happened and was real. It's almost as if Bigfoot wanted me to believe in its existence, and for that I will be forever grateful. The encounter changed my life forever and has made me a strong believer in the potential of the unknown. Maybe one day we'll learn more about this elusive creature but until then all we can do is keep an open mind and hope for the best. Bigfoot might just turn out to be real after all!

ENCOUNTER #24 The Encounter That Changed My Life

It was 1984 and I was living in the south of England. I had gone out for a drive, just to get away from it all for a while. After about an hour of driving, I stopped for a break near a wooded area. It was almost dusk and the sun had started to set, creating a hazy orange glow over the trees.

As I sat there admiring the scenery, something caught my eye -shadowy figure moving among the trees. At first, I assumed it must be a deer or some other woodland creature but as it stepped closer into view, I realized this was no ordinary animal – this was Bigfoot! He stood at least eight feet tall with hair covering his body except for his face, which was black. His eyes were huge and bright red – almost like an animal's in the dark.

I watched, transfixed, as he slowly made his way towards me, stopping just a few feet away from my car window. We stared at each other for what felt like an eternity before he finally took off back into the woods. I could hardly believe what I had seen and couldn't help but feel a wave of emotions – fear, awe, disbelief all rolled into one.

To this day, I still remember that fateful encounter with Big Foot as if it had happened yesterday – from the details of his appearance to the strange feeling of being so close to something so mysterious and unknown. It left me with an indelible feeling that will never be forgotten.

The experience changed me in ways I can't explain and has left me with a newfound appreciation for the unknown and mysterious wonders of nature. To this day, I still love to go out into the countryside and explore, though I have never seen Bigfoot again since that fateful night all those years ago.

ENCOUNTER #25 A Night of Mystery

It was spring of 1988 in the Glastonbury region of Somerset, UK and I had just turned 10 years old. My dad, his best friend and his son who were all about my age had made a fishing trip, so that's where I spent most of my day with them - nestled on a sandbar in the middle of the river.

We had all been there for some time before it happened; we'd built a fire and roasted s'mores over it until late into the night. It must have been around 3am when I woke up with an awful stomach ache, no doubt from eating too much of those sugary treats! I got out of bed to stoke the fire back up again when suddenly I heard something swishing in the water. It sounded as if someone was making their way through the river against the current, heading towards us.

I was immediately filled with a sense of unease. This unknown presence stopped right in front of me - approximately 20 feet away - and reached out to grab one of our two fish baskets. Its head lifted up, its eyes piercing into mine, as if it were saying 'I'm taking these fish, please and thank you'. I froze in place. Then without another word or sound, it walked back downstream with the stolen basket until eventually fading from my sight in the darkness of night.

At first I was too scared to move but gradually my fear turned into awe as I realized what I had just seen - Bigfoot, right here in the UK! After a few minutes I managed to muster up enough courage to go tell my dad. When he woke up we talked about it alone and he told me to keep my encounter a secret until the time was right.

That's exactly what I did until now, more than thirty years later. To this day I remember every detail of that fateful night as if it were yesterday. The creature was tall, at least seven feet, with dark brown fur covering its body and an expression on its face that seemed both mysterious and wise. It stood still for some moments as if studying me before finally making its move away with our fish.

Afterwards, I felt relieved yet strangely excited and still can't believe I had a sighting of Bigfoot in the UK! Such an experience left me with a newfound appreciation of life and a desire to explore and discover more. To this day, I'm still searching for answers about that mysterious creature and all its secrets.

ENCOUNTER #26 A Close Encounter with Bigfoot in London

It was the year 1999 in London, England and I was twelve years old. My brother and I were out on a Sunday afternoon playing in the park when our day suddenly changed forever. We had been there for hours, running around and exploring until the sun started to set.

As we made our way back towards home, something caught my eye that seemed too surreal to be real - It was Bigfoot! He must have been ten feet tall with hair reaching down his arms at least six inches long; it was jet black and matted as if he hadn't groomed himself in weeks. The thing that really stayed with me however were his piercing red eyes which seem to watch us wherever we went.

My brother and I were frozen in shock and fear as this giant creature kept its gaze fixed on us. As our fear began to take over, we started running back home but Bigfoot followed us! It seemed like he was picking up speed and closing the gap between us with each step. We had no choice but to keep running until we finally made it home and slammed the door shut behind us.

When we told our parents what had happened, they didn't believe a single word of it. But when my brother found Bigfoot's tracks in the mud near our house, even they couldn't deny that something strange had definitely been there that day.

The encounter left me feeling uneasy for weeks afterwards, but also strangely fascinated by what I'd seen - a real-life Bigfoot in the UK!

ENCOUNTER #27 The Unexplained Sighting at the Creek

I remember it like it was yesterday. It was a mild spring day in 2020 and I had to work an early morning shift at the factory. As always, I left my house a few minutes before 6am with just enough time to get there for 7am. The sky was still dark but it was so peaceful and quiet as I drove along the country roads.

About 1/2 way to work I passed by a small creek which meandered its way through some woods. I could hear the familiar sound of water running over rocks and something else that shouldn't have been there - movement. As I slowed down to investigate, I saw a tall figure standing on the edge of the creek. It was facing away from me but as soon as I noticed it wasn't a human, I felt my heart start to race.

I quickly moved closer and that's when I saw what it was holding - a fish in its hands which it must have been eating. As soon as our eyes met, the creature dropped the fish into the water and started running away. All I could make out was that it had brown fur and was much larger than an average human being with estimated height and weight around 6 feet 8 inches tall and over 300 pounds! Most importantly, this creature had no tail - so it couldn't have been a bear.

I froze in my car for a few moments, my brain trying to take in what I had just witnessed. Was this really a Bigfoot? A creature that has been talked about for centuries but never truly seen. My heart was beating faster than ever and all I could think of was the need to get back on the road and away from there as fast as possible - which is exactly what I did.

As I sped away, I felt a mix of fear and excitement - had I just seen the mythical creature that has fascinated people for generations? To this day, I have no idea what it was but now always take a different road to work.

ENCOUNTER #28 Encounter With Bigfoot in Scotland

I was camping out with my friend, Jack, near a lake in Scotland on a warm summer night in 2016. We had decided to go camping that weekend as a break from our stressful lives and it seemed like the perfect opportunity for some much needed relaxation. We arrived at our campsite late afternoon and set up our tent and made dinner over an open fire. After eating, we retired to our tent to enjoy some peace and quiet away from civilization.

Little did I know that this peaceful evening would soon become anything but. As we lay down in the tent, we heard loud whoops coming from the woods beyond us. It sounded like something big was stirring around but we weren't sure what it was.

We decided to investigate and stepped out of our tent, turning on our spot light as we did so. What I saw next made my heart skip a beat and I must admit, I nearly pissed my pants in fear. About 10 yards away was a family group of four or five creatures standing around 10 feet tall - the smaller one being about 6 1/2 feet tall. They all screamed and whooped wildly, throwing rocks at us for good measure. It was truly terrifying!

We quickly ran back to the safety of our tent, but not before getting a good look at these creatures - they had dark brown fur covering their entire body with patches of white on their hands and feet. They had large head and their eyes shone brightly in the darkness.

The figures stood there for what seemed like an eternity, staring us down before eventually wandering off into the night. We stayed huddled together in our tent for hours afterwards, too afraid to move or make a sound until dawn broke and we felt safe enough to finally relax.

That experience still haunts me to this day, but I'm so glad I got away unscathed. It was truly an unexpected encounter that I won't soon forget!

ENCOUNTER #29 George's Encounter with Bigfoot

It was June 1995, when George, his 19 year old son Dan, and their dog Daisy ventured out to the woods of Scotland in search of a peaceful weekend away. Little did they know that this trip would change all of their lives forever.

On the second day of their stay, at around 4 pm, Dan was outside playing fetch with Daisy near the edge of the woods. Suddenly he saw something that made him freeze where he stood - it was large and dark-haired, easily over seven feet tall and nearly twice as wide as an average human being. At first glance Dan thought it could have been some kind of bear but when the creature moved closer he could see that it was definitely something else.

The creature seemed to be in no hurry, slowly and cautiously venturing out of the woods and towards Dan. He started to back away, but couldn't take his eyes off it - its size, strength and almost human-like features captivated him. George had heard his son's yell from inside the cabin and ran outside with a flashlight to investigate. When he saw what Dan was looking at he immediately knew what it was - a Bigfoot!

It wasn't until later when they were discussing the experience that George noticed something peculiar about this beast - unlike most Bigfoots sightings which occur during nighttime hours, this one happened broad daylight! This made them both feel even more amazed and intrigued.

The encounter with the Bigfoot lasted maybe a minute or two, before it slowly turned around and walked back into the woods, never to be seen again. After that day, George and Dan's lives would never be the same. They were now part of an elite group of people who could say they had encountered a Bigfoot in the UK - something they thought was impossible!

ENCOUNTER #30 The Day I Quit Fishing

I was on my day off, and had decided to go fishing. This activity has always been a favorite of mine, and so I set out bright and early in the morning with all of my gear. It was late April, just before summer came around; I was walking along a river near London, England.

The morning was peaceful, full of birdsong and occasional bugs buzzing around me. As the minutes ticked by, I began to relax and focus on the task at hand - catching some fish! But then something strange caught my attention: an overwhelming stench filled the air. Wary but still curious, I continued fish until suddenly... BigFoot emerged from the river!

The creature stood just over seven feet tall, and looked to be around 500 pounds. It had matted black hair all over its body and a face that was both human-like and animalistic at the same time. I froze in horror as it lifted a fish out of the water with its powerful hands, gulping it down whole without noticing me.

But then it did notice me, turning towards me slowly. Its eyes were huge and dark; I could feel them boring into my soul as if it was trying to understand my fear. Thankfully, we stared at each other for only a few seconds before BigFoot returned to his business - fishing for food in the river - giving me an opportunity to quickly pack up and run away.

I had never experienced such a powerful emotion before, and it wasn't until I was far away from the river that I finally stopped shaking with fear. This incident has stayed with me ever since, reminding me to always be aware of my surroundings - especially near rivers! Who knows what else lurks in the depths...

ENCOUNTER #31 The Dreadful Encounter With Bigfoot

It was a bright, sunny day in March of 2008 and I had just picked my two kids up from school. We were headed home on a quiet country road near our small town in East Sussex.

As we rounded a sharp corner, we saw something that none of us would ever forget.

There, standing across the road from us was this huge creature – easily 8 feet tall – with black fur covering its body and long arms reaching down to its massive hands. Its head was wide and flat, like that of an ape, but larger than any gorilla I'd ever seen before. My children screamed as soon as they saw it and all I could think to do was hit the accelerator and get away as quickly as possible.

Just before I put my foot on the gas, the creature reacted to our presence and began shuffling towards us. It was close enough for me to see its eyes clearly: they were deep and red, like an animal's but with a hint of something sinister behind them. My kids continued screaming in terror, their little faces pressed against the window glass.

I sped away from the scene, not taking my eyes off the beast until it had disappeared from view.

The terrifying encounter ended up lasting no more than 15 seconds, but that short time felt like a lifetime – especially for my children who had nightmares filled with this large black creature for months afterwards. I still have no idea what we saw that day, but I know it wasn't something from this world.

It had been a long time since I'd heard any reports of Bigfoot in the UK and the thought of one being so close to our home filled me with dread. Thankfully, nobody was hurt during our encounter, but the memory still fills us with fear whenever we drive by that same stretch of road.

Though we were lucky to have made it out unscathed, this harrowing experience will stay with us forever. The Dreadful Encounter With Bigfoot in the UK is a story no one should ever have to tell – but for our family it's now one we'll never forget.

ENCOUNTER #32 A 12 Year Old's Story of Bigfoot

It was a cold autumn night in 1988. My family had recently moved to a small rural village just outside of London, and I was trying to get used to our new home. That night, I was trying to fall asleep in my bedroom when something strange caught my eye. As the moonlight streamed through my window, I could make out two large eyes peering into the room from outside!

I immediately screamed for help and started calling for my dad. He came running into my bedroom and turned on the lights to find me trembling with fear but nothing else amiss - whatever it was seemed to have disappeared. Dad thought that I had imagined it, and tried to reassure me that everything was ok. But the next morning, he noticed a huge footprint outside my window that none of us could recognize.

We couldn't believe our eyes. The footprint was large - about two feet long and one foot wide - with distinct ridges on the sole, almost like there were five toes! We knew we weren't dealing with a regular animal or person, so we began asking around the village for any similar reports. Sure enough, people had been talking about mysterious sightings in our area for quite some time now.

My dad decided to do some research into what this creature could be, and after reading up on various folklore tales and local legends, he eventually arrived at a conclusion - it was a Bigfoot!

We were skeptical at first, but after talking to some of the other villagers who had similar stories, we started to believe.

They told us that this creature had been spotted multiple times across different parts of the UK - usually in remote locations and usually at night. People described it as being around seven feet tall with dark fur, and wide eyes which shone in the moonlight like mine had. It seemed like what I'd seen was not just a myth - but an actual living breathing creature!

Though we couldn't be sure about what happened that night, it left me feeling shaken up for weeks afterwards. While I'm glad nothing bad happened, I still get shivers down my spine when I think of that moment. I'm now more sure than ever that there's something out there that remains unexplained - a mysterious creature lurking in the shadows, watching from afar. Even to this day, I still can't help but wonder - did I really see a Bigfoot? What else could it have been?

ENCOUNTER #33 A Camping Trip to Remember

It was the summer of 2011, and a group of friends from London had decided to take a weekend camping trip in the Scottish Highlands. We were all 18 years old and so excited for our first ever camping experience without parents.

We spent the day prior to the encounter exploring some of the hiking trails in the area, taking pictures, and talking about exciting plans for our campfire later that night. We arrived at our campsite with plenty of time before sundown and started setting up our tents.

That night we heard loud thudding noises against our tent as if something was throwing rocks or small stones at us while we slept inside. We quickly got out of bed and went outside to investigate but saw nothing. We thought it was just some local kids messing around and decided to go back inside and get some rest.

The next day, we were out exploring the woods near our campsite when we heard a loud howl coming from high up on a hill. We immediately looked up and saw what looked like a tall dark figure walking quickly away up the hillside. We couldn't believe our eyes! We knew instantly that this must have been Big Foot in Scotland - something that we had only ever seen in movies before! We were filled with shock and fear so quickly packed up our things and left the area as fast as possible. It was an experience that none of us will ever forget.

ENCOUNTER #34 Bike Chain Encounter

The day started out like any other in the small town of Inverness, Scotland. It was a beautiful summer morning and I had just turned 15 years old. Me, my dad and my brother decided to take a ride on our bikes along the rolling hills of northern Scotland. We had been biking for hours when I noticed that my bike chain had come off again, so I stopped to try to adjust it.

I looked up from where I was kneeling and saw something strange in the distance. My dad and brother also stopped and we all stared at what appeared to be a giant figure standing about 500 meters away from us. As we studied the creature more closely we could see it was almost 8 feet tall with thick black hair covering its body. Its eyes were like two burning coals and it was utterly motionless as if it were studying us just as we studied it.

My heart raced, fear freezing me in place, but I felt no malice emanating from the creature. It seemed to be observing us with a kind of curiosity. We all stayed rooted to our spots for what must have been five minutes before my dad started calling out and waving his hands in the air. After a few moments, the creature slowly turned around and ambled away into the nearby woods without ever making a sound.

The experience left us all shaken yet strangely exhilarated. We watched until the figure disappeared into the trees, not sure of what had just happened or if we would ever see it again.

ENCOUNTER #35 I Saw Bigfoot Coming Home From Work

It was summertime, and I had just turned 25. I was home for the summer from university and decided to take a job close to home so I could spend more time with my parents. Little did I know that this decision would lead me to an encounter of a lifetime.

That fateful afternoon, I left work feeling exhausted after a long shift. Despite being tired, I felt excited for the lovely walk home through the woods near our house. As soon as I entered the woods, something felt off - almost like someone was watching me from afar. The feeling continued until eventually, it became too strong to ignore any longer.

I stopped in my tracks and looked around. I noticed a large, shadowy figure in the distance. It was difficult to make out any features from so far away but I could tell it was tall - at least seven or eight feet tall - and had long, dark brown fur.

I felt a wave of fear wash over me as I realized what this figure could be. I'd heard stories about bigfoot sightings here in the UK, but until that moment had never thought they were real. As I watched, the figure seemed to notice me too and it began to move towards me.

I wanted to run away but my feet were frozen in place with fear. After what felt like an eternity, the creature suddenly stopped and looked around cautiously before turning around and disappearing back into the woods.

I was left feeling a mix of relief and disbelief. Could I really have just seen bigfoot? After a few minutes, I continued my walk home and spent the rest of the evening debating whether or not to tell anyone about what had happened. Despite being almost three years ago now, that day is still as clear in my mind as it was back then. To this day, I'm still convinced I encountered the mysterious beast that summer afternoon in the UK woods.

ENCOUNTER #36 Romantic Walk Turned Terrifying

It was a sunny summer day in 2016 and my then girlfriend, now wife and I decided to take a romantic walk through the woods near London. We had already done many walks here before and nothing out of ordinary had ever happened so we felt safe, with no need for concern. Little did we know that this would soon change.

We were about halfway through our walk, walking hand-in-hand down the trail when suddenly something whizzed past us and landed on the other side of the path. Before either of us could react another rock followed it and landed at our feet. We both looked around startled only to be met by silence. That's when we heard rustling in the woods and saw a figure about eight feet tall, covered in brown fur. We knew it could only be one thing: Bigfoot.

We were paralyzed with fear and couldn't believe what we were seeing. The creature was throwing rocks at us, as if trying to scare us off. It lifted its head up so that its face was visible, it had two round eyes facing directly at us and an angry look on its face. That's when we snapped out of our trance and ran back to our car as quickly as possible.

Afterwards we felt shaken up but grateful that nothing worse had happened to us during this encounter with bigfoot. Although we don't know why it threw rocks at us, we will never forget our first and only encounter with Bigfoot in the UK.

ENCOUNTER #37 The Pizza Run

It was a cool, autumn evening in 1995 or 1996. My friend and I had been out for a bite to eat earlier in the day, picking up some pizza before heading back towards his house. The sun had already set by this time so we found ourselves traveling along a road that was shrouded in darkness. This particular stretch of road consisted of two lanes with a berm running alongside it - about three feet lower than the fields adjacent to it. As we rounded the corner, my friend and I spotted something ahead in the distance.

We could see that it was large and dark-colored - towering over us as our car slowly approached. We were both intrigued by the figure and stopped to take a better look. As our car crept closer, we both peered out of the sunroof - and that is when I saw it.

Standing before us was an enormous creature, its head easily towering over the road. From what I could make out in the dim lighting, it seemed to be around 8 feet tall and slightly overweight, with short brown fur covering its body. Its eyes glowed bright in the darkness as we stared in awe at this unexpected sighting. We were both so surprised by what we had just seen that neither of us said a word - we just drove off in silence and never spoke about it again for fear of people thinking we were crazy.

I still remember that evening and the incredible feeling it gave us. As I look back, it's almost surreal to think that something like Bigfoot could exist in the UK - but we both saw it and there was no denying it.

To this day, I still can't believe my friend and I encountered Bigfoot in the UK on that dark autumn night. It was a moment that will be forever etched into my memory - an experience that neither of us will ever forget.

ENCOUNTER #38 Mary & I's Encounter with Bigfoot

It was a crisp autumn day in October of 2018 when my friend Mary and I decided to take a walk through the woods of Northumberland, England. We had always heard tales of mysterious creatures lurking around these parts, but we never expected to actually see one! As we strolled along, admiring the beautiful foliage, we suddenly noticed something huge far off in the distance. At first, we thought it might be a deer or wild boar due to its size and shape; however after staring at it for what seemed like forever, it suddenly got up on two legs and began walking away from us!

We both gasped as we realized that this couldn't possibly have been a deer, bear or boar. We were both in shock and immediately began to speculate as to what this creature could have been. Mary exclaimed, "At first I thought it was a strange bear, but when it stood up on two legs and began walking away like a man, I knew we were seeing something out of the ordinary!"

As we continued walking forward cautiously, the figure disappeared into the woods. We had found ourselves face-to-face with Bigfoot! We estimated its height to be around 8 feet tall and it seemed to weigh somewhere between 250-300 pounds. Its body was covered in long fur that was dark brown in color with streaks of gray throughout. All we could really make out from our far away vantage point were its eyes, which seemed to be a pale yellow in color.

The encounter lasted no more than two minutes, but we were both left feeling stunned and slightly shaken afterwards. A creature like this shouldn't exist, yet somehow it did! We had encountered Bigfoot right here in the UK; something that we never expected ever to experience. Who knows what other creatures may be lurking around these parts that we don't even know about?

This was an experience that will stay with us forever, and one that definitely proved that sometimes even the most unbelievable things actually exist. We still tell our story of encountering Bigfoot in Northumberland to anyone who'll listen - you better believe it!

ENCOUNTER #39 My Encounter with Bigfoot in the UK

It was an unusual sunny day in 2012, and my husband and I had decided to take a break from our busy lives and go camping near the River Severn in Gloucestershire. We woke up early that morning and started setting up camp. We were both excited for the peacefulness of nature, so we explored the area around us throughout the day.

In the afternoon as my husband went down to get water from the river, I heard a loud crash of a tree falling nearby. Just after that I heard three knocks followed by three more coming from across the river – it sounded like someone or something was trying to communicate! A few times later we also heard some snorts and howls coming from the trees. We were both intrigued, so after dinner we started talking about what could have made that noise.

That's when I first became aware of the possibility of Bigfoot in the UK. We laughed it off at first, but then my husband said he had read some stories on a blog where people claimed to have seen it in this area before and told me about it. He got into the tent and told me about it. We talked for a couple minutes before saying good night.

Less than 5 minutes after we stopped talking we both heard rustling in the leaves from a distance, we both lifted our heads and listened intently as the footsteps came closer. We both agree the footsteps were in two's, it was a patterned walking. We were frozen in fear as the footsteps kept getting louder and closer until it sounded like it was right behind our tent! We both lay completely still, not daring to move an inch or make any noise. It seemed to walk around the campfire ring and then off into the woods towards the water.

As soon as the sound faded away I began shaking uncontrollably! I have never felt fear like that before and had never reacted to fear that way. My husband was trying to reassure me when we heard it returning about 2 minutes later. I grabbed my key fab for our van and hit the lock button so that lights would light up, hopefully scaring away whatever it was. The footsteps stopped and there was silence!

We heard what sounded like a fight going on between two animals in that direction, so I hit the lights again a couple of times and the noises stopped. We knew we wouldn't be able to sleep in the tent anymore so we moved into our van for the rest of the night.

The next morning, my husband and I were both exhausted but eager to find out if it had been Bigfoot or not. We searched around for tracks and evidence but couldn't find anything except some broken branches near where it had been standing when we last saw it. We never found any more signs of Bigfoot but what we did see left us with an overwhelming sense of awe and amazement.

ENCOUNTER #40 It Was A Brutal Winter Night

It was the winter of 2009 and it was freezing. I had just finished up a long day of work and decided to take our dog for a walk before bed. I was living in the small rural town of Howdon, located in North Tyneside, with my parents at the time. It was around midnight when I got home from work and started to get our dog ready for his nightly stroll. I should've known something strange was about to happen when the dog started growling aggressively as soon as he heard me coming

At first, I thought that maybe there was just some sort of animal or creature outside that he didn't like the smell of, but I quickly realized that there was something else out there. As we started to walk down the road, I could feel a strange presence in the air and it made my skin crawl with fear. For about a minute or so I started to smell a rather odd oder. It's was one like I had never smelt before. It was musky and pungent and just completely odd where we were at.

I mentioned all the wildlife we had in the area because I had been around all of. And none of those animals ever had a smell like this. That's when the neighbors dogs who had been barking like mad suddenly went completely quiet and my dog who had been growling nonstop suddenly stopped. I knew something was up but my mind couldn't comprehend what it could be at the time. Moments later I heard a loud thud and then a shuffling of feet that got louder and louder as time went on.

As I started to get closer and closer to the sound, I felt a sense of dread come over me and although I wanted to turn around and run for help, my body wouldn't let me do so because of the sheer curiosity that filled my veins. That's when I saw it walking through an open field about 100-120 yards away from us. It was massive in size; standing at least 8ft tall and very muscular in build. The creature was covered in long, dark brown fur and had a long face with two glowing eyes. I couldn't believe what I was seeing!

I'm not sure how long the encounter lasted but it felt like hours. We stayed frozen in fear as we watched the creature walk across the field and eventually disappear into the night. After it was gone, all of my fear seemed to evaporate and I felt strangely calm despite what my mind had just witnessed. It was one of the most bizarre things that has ever happened to me and although I'll never know for sure if what we saw that night truly was a Bigfoot, its something that will stay with me forever.

ENCOUNTER #41 Bigfoot in Blakemere Woods

It was a cold, dreary Tuesday evening in the summer of 2014 and I had just finished work at around 8pm. A group of us from the office decided to go for a walk along Blakemere Woods outside Manchester before heading home for the day. We were all laughing, joking and chatting away when I began to get an uneasy feeling. At first I brushed it off as being tired but then my friend stopped abruptly, looking around with wide eyes like they'd seen a ghost.

"What is it?" I asked nervously, not sure what could have caused such a reaction in them. It was then that I heard it - heavy footsteps thudding through the trees towards us, echoing off into the darkness. Instinctively, the group of us huddled closer together as we strained our eyes to make out what could have been making such a racket.

That is when it revealed itself - standing at around 9 feet tall and covered in thick, matted brown fur was Bigfoot, its large yellow eyes shining eerily in the moonlight. The creature seemed unfazed by our presence and instead continued pacing around us, seemingly mimicking each step we took. We froze with fear as none of us knew what to do. It felt like an eternity before Big Foot finally stopped moving, slowly turning away from us before vanishing back into the shadows of the woods.

The encounter with Bigfoot had lasted only a few minutes but it felt much longer than that. We all stood there in stunned silence, before eventually regaining our composure and making our way back home. Although we were scared at the time, the experience has left us with a sense of awe and wonder about this mysterious creature that inhabits the British countryside.

ENCOUNTER #42 Jogging Through the UK Woods

It was a sunny day in 2018, and I had just finished an afternoon jog around the village in South East England. Feeling invigorated by the fresh air, I decided to take a longer route home and continued through some nearby woods.

Little did I know that this would soon become one of the most frightening experiences of my life. It all started when I began to feel like something was following me from within

115

the depths of the trees; at first it felt like an eerie chill up my spine but then it became more than that - a feeling of imminent danger. Taking out my earphones, I heard movement echoing my own footsteps - something was definitely pacing me.

Paralyzed with fear, I quickly turned around and that is when I saw it. Standing in the shadows at what seemed like a safe enough distance of around 15 feet away, was a tall hulking figure with thick brown fur covering its body. Its face was covered by even thicker fur and its eyes were glowing bright yellow in the waning afternoon light.

I couldn't believe that I had stumbled across Bigfoot right here in the UK! My heart raced as we stared at each other for what felt like an eternity before finally he broke his gaze and slowly stepped back into the trees.

Afterwards, I could hardly believe what had happened; my hands were still trembling as I made my way back to the village, my mind racing with questions. Where did he come from? How long had he been following me for?

I'm still having trouble grasping that I came across a real-life Bigfoot in South East England, but I know one thing for certain: I will never forget this terrifying encounter.

ENCOUNTER #43 The Day I Saw Bigfoot

It was a cool summer day in the highlands of Scotland. I had been camping alone for three days, just looking to get away from it all and enjoy some peace and quiet in nature. Little did I know that my peaceful trip would be interrupted by an encounter with something entirely unexpected.

On the third evening, as the sun was starting to set, I noticed several trees that seemed out of place - they were uprooted and shoved back into the ground with their tops pointing down into the earth and their roots exposed. It was strange, but I couldn't think of anything that could have caused this phenomenon.

As I continued my walk I noticed something even more peculiar - a set of huge footprints in the mud. They definitely weren't from any animal that I'd ever seen, and they were too big to be human. Shaken, but still curious, I followed the tracks for a short while until darkness started to fall.

That's when things got really strange. At first it was faint, but soon enough I heard a loud knocking sound coming from deep within the woods. As terrified as I was, my curiosity got the better of me and I decided to investigate further into the forest without considering any potential danger lurking around me.

I didn't see anything at first, but then suddenly out of nowhere there it was: Bigfoot! He was enormous, at least 10 feet tall and weighing close to 500 pounds. He had dark, shaggy fur all over his body and he was walking slowly in my direction.

My heart raced as I watched him, but then suddenly he stopped and looked right at me. We stared into each others' eyes for what felt like an eternity before he calmly turned around and walked away without making a sound.

The encounter lasted no more than five minutes, but it left me feeling shaken and overwhelmed with emotion. I couldn't believe that I had just seen Bigfoot! It was the summer of 2018 in the highlands of Scotland and I will never forget that day.

ENCOUNTER #44 Saved By a Female Bigfoot

It was a crisp autumn day in the heart of London, England; I and my childhood friends -- John, Sarah, and Mark -- were walking through Hyde Park on our way home. We had spent hours playing tag in the park and were feeling exhausted. The sun had started to set and it was getting dark, so we decided that it was time to leave. Little did we know what awaited us just around the corner!

We heard a loud noise coming from behind some bushes, like something heavy falling onto the ground with a thud. Startled by the sound, we slowly looked up in the direction of where it came from. And that is when we saw her: a female Bigfoot! She was about 8 feet tall and covered in black fur, with a muscular build. We were all frozen in place; I remember feeling my heart beat faster as I stared at the giant creature standing before us.

Just then, a male Bigfoot emerged out of nowhere, coming to stand next to his female companion. He seemed huge and imposing compared to her -- almost 10 feet tall! Seeing this, we felt even more scared than before; what would they do? To our surprise however, the female bigfoot acted quickly and stepped between us and the male. Her body language suggested that she was trying to protect us from him. As if by some instinctive understanding, we did not move or make any sound for fear of provoking him. The female bigfoot seemed to sense our fear, for she kept calm and simply stared at us until the male eventually backed away and disappeared into the darkness.

As soon as he was out of sight, we all ran in opposite directions towards home. We were so relieved that nothing bad had happened to us -- all thanks to the female Bigfoot! To this day, I still remember that incredible encounter with both amazement and reverence; it will forever remain imprinted in my memory.

ENCOUNTER #45 Bigfoot Kills a Red Deer

It was a cold, dark autumn evening in 2004 when my brother and I set out to explore the serene woods of Scotland. We had both grown up loving stories of myths and legends surrounding these old grounds — such as tales of Big Foot — so it was with excitement that we ventured through the tall trees and lush ferns, hoping to catch a glimpse ourselves.

We spent hours wandering around, marveling at the beauty of nature while snacking on our picnic lunch. Eventually we settled down against an old fallen tree trunk to take a break before continuing home. It was then that I happened to glance up into the distance and saw something quite extraordinary: what appeared to be a Bigfoot.

I remember my brother and I both froze in shock, unsure of what we were witnessing. The creature was huge — estimated at around 8 feet tall — and covered in a thick dark brown fur. It seemed to move with ease despite its size, galloping swiftly after a red deer that had caught its attention. The bigfoot kept pace with the animal effortlessly, eventually catching up to it and killing it outright. We watched from afar for what felt like an eternity before we realized this wasn't something we wanted to stick around for; so my brother grabbed our bags and we started running back towards home as soon as possible.

The whole incident left us feeling quite shaken and disturbed - especially knowing that such a creature existed and just how close we had been to it without even realizing. We both made sure to keep the story of our experience a secret — not wanting anyone else to have the same fate as us. It's now something that I still think about today whenever I hear stories of bigfoot - and will remain etched in my memory forever.

ENCOUNTER #46 Scared After Moving

It was the summer of 1987 and my family and I had just moved from London to a small town in southern England. My dad got a new job, so we all loaded up our things and made the big move into our new home. I was 11 years old at the time, excited for this fresh start but a little unsure about how different it would be living in rural England compared to London.

I quickly found out that there were plenty of trails around town for me to explore with my mountain bike. Every day after school, I'd rush outside before homework and go on expeditions throughout the countryside, seeing what sights I could stumble upon.

One afternoon while biking along one familiar trail next to the river, I stopped to get a drink of water and I noticed out of the corner of my eye something walking out from behind the trees. At first, I couldn't believe what I was seeing-- it looked like a man, but much taller than any person I'd ever seen before. It stood at least 8 feet tall with large features and powerful arms. Its skin was covered in thick fur in shades of brown and gray, and its face had deep wrinkles that gave off an aura of wisdom.

The creature seemed to be preoccupied with something outside of my presence; it clicked its tongue rapidly as if communicating with someone or something else out there. As soon as I made a move to go, the creature's mood shifted abruptly and it let out a loud growl directed right at me. I froze in fear, scared of what would happen next.

Suddenly, I heard more clicking and growling coming from the other side of the trees and another creature appeared! It was identical to the first except that it seemed much angrier. In sheer panic, I got back on my bike and raced away as fast as I could until the sound of their voices were no longer audible.

That summer day changed my life forever; I'd seen something that didn't seem possible-- bigfoot in England! To this day I can still remember how scared yet intrigued I felt during this encounter. A Memory of Bigfoot Sighting in Southern England.

ENCOUNTER #47 Witnessed by an 8-Year-Old

We were camping near the forests of Northumberland, England. It was a warm summer day in 2003, and my family had decided to take a trip to explore the area and set up camp. I was only 8 years old, but I was already quite excited for our adventure.

Our campsite included two tents, some chairs, a fire pit and cooking supplies. We'd been out walking around earlier that morning and had just returned to eat lunch when it happened. All of a sudden we heard rustling coming from nearby trees – way too loud to be any kind of animal we knew of. I remember being scared, but also curious and excited.

We all froze in place, looking around for the source of the noise. Then, out of nowhere, we saw a large figure walking across our campsite. It was at least 7 feet tall and covered in dark fur – it was unmistakably Bigfoot! We had no idea what to do – we were so shocked and scared that all we could do was stare.

Bigfoot moved slowly, like he had been watching us for some time. He stopped about 15 yards away from us, as if sizing us up. As far as I know, none of us ever made a sound or tried to back away – there was something strange but almost beautiful about this creature standing before us.

The encounter must have lasted about a minute, but it felt like forever. Eventually, Bigfoot started to walk away slowly until he disappeared into the trees. We continued looking in that direction for a few minutes before finally gathering our things and quickly leaving the campsite – I don't think any of us had ever run so fast!

Since that day I've always been fascinated by Bigfoot, especially since it's rare to hear stories of encounters within the UK. Even after all these years, I can still remember every detail as if it happened yesterday - the feeling of surprise, fear and awe I experienced will stay with me forever.

ENCOUNTER #48 Friends Encounter Bigfoot

It was the summer of 2014, and my friends and I had just finished our final exams. We were feeling restless and wanted to take a trip somewhere new. We decided to explore the UK, so we loaded up our RV with supplies and set off on an adventure.

After days of travelling around Scotland, Wales, Ireland, and England, we finally chose one particular spot near a remote lake in northern England as our campsite for the night. Little did we know that this would be a night none of us would ever forget.

We set up camp in the fading light of dusk, enjoying the peaceful atmosphere that surrounded us. Night quickly fell upon us, so we settled ourselves into the RV for some much needed shut-eye.

Suddenly, in the middle of the night, we felt a strong shaking that rocked our RV to its core. We awoke with a start and quickly scrambled out of bed. Our hearts racing, we slowly opened the door to find out what was causing all this commotion.

Peering into the darkness, I saw something odd just beyond the clearing. It seemed to be sitting on two legs and looking right at us! I couldn't tell exactly how tall it was but it seemed quite big. Its fur was dark brown and its eyes were bright yellow! We watched in amazement as whatever it was started running away from us towards the woods nearby.

We stood there for a few moments, trying to take in what just happened. It felt like an eternity before we finally decided to go back into the RV and try to get some much needed rest.

The next morning, we all awoke with a feeling of uneasiness but also awe that something as mysterious as Bigfoot had chosen our campsite for its nightly activities. We never got a good look at it, yet there was no doubt in our minds that this creature existed.

We packed up our belongings and left the campground shortly after sunrise, still buzzed from the previous night's events.

ENCOUNTER #49 Our Unforgettable Encounter

It was a warm summer day in 2012, and my girlfriend and I had decided to take a hike near Dartmoor National Park located in Devon, England. We were excited to explore the area, which we'd heard was full of some truly amazing wildlife and scenery. Little did we know that this seemingly normal day would become unforgettable.

We didn't get far into our journey before we started hearing an odd sound - a loud grunt coming from down the trail about thirty feet away from us. Instinctively I stopped in my tracks and glanced around warily, not wanting to put either of us in danger. My girlfriend grasped my arm tightly as if knowing what I was thinking without saying it aloud. The grunting continued for about five minutes as we stood there and listened, neither of us moving a muscle.

Eventually the noise stopped and we decided to continue our journey, despite being a bit on edge. We continued further down the trail until it became thicker and denser with trees, tall enough that they blocked out the sunlight from above us. We stood in silence for about five minutes before I noticed something moving in the trees on our left - about twenty feet away. Not wanting to take any chances, I removed my machete and handed my girlfriend her knife which was only six inches long but better than nothing. I took the lead as she held onto me tightly with her left hand while we made our way through the thicket.

That's when we heard it again - the same loud grunt from before, but this time much closer. We both froze in fear and my heart was pounding in my chest. I felt like there was no way we were making it out of here alive. Suddenly a foul smell filled the air around us, similar to wet dog mixed with trash, and we knew that something wasn't right. With tears forming in her eyes my girlfriend pleaded with me to turn back, but I knew that would be impossible at this point as we had walked quite far into the woods already.

So instead I held onto her for reassurance and made sure she stayed close behind me as we continued on our path towards whatever awaited us ahead. As we made our way around the next bend, we were shocked by what we saw. About fifteen feet away from us stood a creature that can only be described as Bigfoot - it was enormous! It must have been at least eight and a half feet tall, with dark brown fur covering its entire body. Its face was long and slender with two small black eyes and a large snout. For what seemed like forever we simply stared in stunned silence, neither of us being able to move or fully process what we were witnessing.

Eventually I heard my girlfriend whisper "What do we do?" As if on cue the creature let out another loud grunt before turning its back towards us and disappearing into the trees. We both let out sighs of relief before retreating back down the same path we came, being sure to keep our eyes on the trees at all times. Once we found ourselves back in the open again, I took my girlfriend's hand and gave it a gentle squeeze. We had encountered Bigfoot that day and lived to tell about it!

ENCOUNTER #50 Mystified by Curiosity

I remember it like it was yesterday, though nearly five decades have passed. It was the late 1960s and I was a young girl living in the United Kingdom. I had been exploring the woods with my friends near our hometown of Exeter, when we had an unexpected encounter with something truly extraordinary – Bigfoot!

We were just kids at the time, no more than 16 years old, so none of us were prepared for what happened that day. We'd spent much of the morning playing in the forest and gathering stones to take home as souvenirs from our adventure. Little did we know that this trip would turn out to be far different from what we expected.

As the afternoon began to draw to a close, we were heading back home when something caught my eye. At first I thought it was just an animal, but as it emerged from behind a tree I realized that this was no ordinary creature. It stood about 7 feet tall and had a stocky build, with dark brown fur covering its entire body. Its face was remarkably human-like, with piercing eyes that looked right into me. For a moment, time seemed to stand still as we all stared at one another in shock – then suddenly the creature turned and disappeared into the woods without making a sound.

We were frozen in place for what felt like an eternity before finally regaining our composure. We quickly decided to head back home and tell no one of what we had seen.

That day changed my life forever. Though I often wonder what happened to that mysterious creature, I will never forget the awe and amazement I felt at the time. To this day, it still lingers in my mind - a reminder of our unexpected encounter with Bigfoot in the UK.

ENCOUNTER #51 It Followed Us Back to Camp

It was the summer of 2009 and we were camping in the woods near Exmoor, England. My little brother Jacob and I had gone out fishing that morning, hoping to catch a few trout for dinner. We had been at it since sunrise but hadn't caught anything yet when headed back to camp in mid-afternoon.

We were about halfway back when I noticed something strange off in the distance. I stopped dead in my tracks and grabbed my binoculars to get a better look. What I saw sent shivers down my spine - there, standing amongst the trees just a few hundred yards away, was an enormous humanoid creature with dark brown fur! It was huge - easily over 10 feet tall!

Jacob spotted it too and we both froze. We were scared out of our wits. I had heard stories about Bigfoot in the UK but this was unexpected by either of us!

The creature seemed to be watching us, as though trying to figure out what we were up to. It didn't move but its eyes followed us intently and it occasionally bared its teeth at us. That's when I noticed the sheer size of those teeth - they looked razor sharp!

We finally found the courage to continue back towards camp. The bigfoot continued to watch us, pacing our footsteps and keeping a distance of about 200 yards away from us. We were too scared to take our eyes off of it until we had made it all the way back to camp, at which point it disappeared into the woods.

When we got back to camp, I immediately told my parents what had happened. They didn't believe us at first but when they saw how pale and shaken up we were they soon realized something remarkable had happened that day.

Ever since then, Jacob and I have often talked about that encounter with Bigfoot in Exmoor - even after all these years, just thinking about it still gives me goosebumps!

Conclusion

As you finish this book, you may be left with more questions than answers about Bigfoot sightings in the UK. But one thing is for sure - these stories have left a lasting impression on you. You've heard firsthand accounts of people who encountered something mysterious and extraordinary in the wilds of Britain, and those tales will stay with you forever.

What do all these stories mean? Are they simply tall tales or could there actually be some truth to them? That's up to you to decide — but one thing we know for certain is that when it comes to mysteries like Bigfoot, nothing can ever be taken for granted!

We hope this book has been an enjoyable journey through the strange world of Bigfoot sightings in the UK. As you go out into the forests, moors and mountains of Britain, we wish you a safe and adventurous trip. Who knows what you might encounter along the way!

Printed in Great Britain
by Amazon